The 7 AHA!s

of Highly Enlightened Souls

How to free yourself from ALL forms of
stress and learn to live your life
peacefully, lovingly, and happily

BOOKS

Winchester, UK.
New York, U.S.A.

Copyright © 2003 O Books

46A West Street, Alresford, Hants SO24 9AU, UK

Tel: +44 (0) 1962 736880 Fax: +44 (0) 1962 736881

E-mail: office@johnhunt-publishing.com

www.o-books.net

USA and Canada

Books available from:

New Book Network

15200 NBN Way

Blue Ridge Summit, PA 17214, USA

Tel: 1 800 462 6420

Fax: 1 800 338 4550

E-mail: custserv@nbnbooks.com

Text: © 2003 Mike George

Designed by Krave Limited

ISBN 1 903816 31 9

Reprinted 2003, 2004, 2005

A CIP catalogue record for this book is available from the British Library.

Printed in the U.K. by Ashford Colour Press

dedication

*To those who are just plain tired of living lives
increasingly filled with stress,
and are ready to 'wake up' and
stop creating their own suffering!*

If you have any questions regarding any
of the ideas/insights in this book
please ask me at
mike@relax7.com

For further insights, visualisations and meditations visit
The Relaxation Centre
www.relax7.com

contents

Section One
Illusion and Myth
The 7 Prevailing Myths about Stress

Section Two
Wisdom and Truth
The 7 Essential Insights into Your Self

Section Three
Action and Transformation
The 7 AHAs of Highly Enlightened Souls

Preface

The Red Thread

Every good book, like every good course, will have an underlying theme, something called the 'red thread', which ties it all together. The red thread of this little book is a simple but vital idea known as self-responsibility.

Regardless of how comfortable people think they are in their life today almost everyone is suffering in some way every day. This is simply because the vast majority have not fully realized and integrated the principle of self-responsibility. All suffering is self-created, regardless of history or circumstances. But you may not know that, or want to know that. Some people know but don't want to live it. Others know it but deny it. The vast majority does not know it, and when they hear it the majority of that majority does not want to believe it...at first!

I know this from the thousands of people I meet every year in seminars, lectures, and workshops around the world. I also know from personal experience that regardless of your past, nothing can change in your life for the better, until you take full responsibility for your self, for your thoughts, emotions, personality, and actions, right now, today. It sounds like a harsh instruction, but in reality it is more like an essential insight into successful and contented living.

Accepting responsibility for your self, for your life experience and your life's destiny is no small step if you have been taught, as most of us have, to believe others are responsible. In becoming self-responsible it is not that we cut ourselves off and live in isolation, narcissistically focussing only on our own needs and wants. The paradox of self-responsibility is that it is a necessity precisely because we live as part of community. And whether it is the community of our home, our work or our world, our impact on that community begins with the degree to which we accept responsibility for our self. If we make the community and our circumstances responsible for our thoughts and actions, if we point the finger of blame for how and what we feel, we are in that moment abdicating from our own life and teaching others an illusion.

I can hear your pain. I know your suffering. This book is a response to your call. It is written for you and to you. It will not answer every question, clarify every confusion or cure every ailment, but it may help you take one small step towards reclaiming your first responsibility, which is your ability to choose your response to life, the universe, and everything!

Mike George, 2003

Introduction

A Time for Transformation

A billion ideas, a million books, thousands of seminars, and hundreds of modern-day enlightenment gurus have all exploded on to the world in the last two decades to help us restore some wisdom and wonder to our busy lives.

Their mission is to teach us how to chill and stay chilled. They are trying to show us how to take back control of our destiny and how to be better human beings in a world of people perpetually doing! They have come to tell us that we are essentially asleep to who we are and why we are here. They have found numerous ways to remind us that we can easily live our entire lives unaware of the true beauty within each of us, and the creative opportunity which each of our lives represent.

You may have noticed, however, that there is no course, seminar, book, or guru that can actually change or transform your life. Transformation is a frequent promise, but it is a promise that is impossible to deliver. Why? Because only you can do the work of waking up and staying awake. Only you can change the way you think, feel, and live. All the techniques, tools, and methods in the world are of little value unless you are motivated and ready to do the inner work of awakening to the illusions that keep you stuck in patterns of lazy thinking, false beliefs, and distorted perceptions. And although you may not be aware, although you may think your thinking, believing, and perceiving is just fine thank you, each and every one of us needs to do some inner work at this level.

The purpose of this little book is to give you the basic insights and inner methods to free yourself from the most prevalent illusions that keep us trapped in our habits of negative and lazy thinking. The aim is to help you to see, challenge, and release the false beliefs that keep you stuck in stressful patterns of behavior. The goal is to help you see how you can choose more positive perceptions and create more positive, heart-healthy feelings. And one of the objectives is to help you to reawaken your awareness of your true self, as opposed to the self you have learned from others, as you embark on your own path to personal enlightenment.

However, while this book is packed with insights, self-help methods and occasional wisdom, none of these will have any real value until you see truth, see the wisdom, for yourself, within yourself. This moment of "seeing" or realization is known as the AHA! moment.

THE AHA! MOMENT

We have all had an AHA! moment. It is a moment of profound insight into some problem you have been struggling to resolve, or a flash of clarity about a difficult situation that you are facing.

In the moment of the AHA! you are suddenly blessed, for no apparent reason, with a realization of what is exactly the right thing to do or say (or not, as the case may be). Not only that, but you are absolutely sure it is the perfect answer. You do not need to think about it. In fact, if you do think about it, you immediately begin to diminish its power.

The AHA! moment, or as some have described it, the "eureka experience", usually comes when you cease to struggle mentally and intellectually for solutions or answers to a perceived problem or challenge. Your mind and intellect are relaxed, open, and receptive to new ways of seeing. For thousands of years, meditation has been the acknowledged method to clear the internal clutter and quieten the noise of thoughts and feelings, which then allows the AHA! moment to arrive. However, quiet moments of introspection and reflection can also provide a silent space for the dawn of a new vision that also brings with it a surge in your personal power.

Most inventors will testify to the AHA! moment as the breakthrough to seeing exactly how their new creation will take shape. Numerous scientists will recall times when an AHA! moment was the first fresh impulse in the formulation of a new theory. And many successful business people will happily tell of an uninvited AHA! heralding a crucial business decision, or completely new direction, which then contributed much to their success.

AHA! moments can change your life and the lives of others. May there be at least one and perhaps many AHA!s for you in this book. And may you act on each one instantly. For only in action lies their power to affect change for the better in your life.

Section One

Illusion and Myth

The Seven Prevailing Myths about Stress

Is This Little Book Really for You?

The 20th-century disease called "stress" is now a 21st-century epidemic – and it kills.

More and more people are beginning to do something about it. Business and industry are slowly awakening to the fact that billions of yen, dollars, euros, and pounds are lost every year in absenteeism, inefficiency, relationship conflict, and poor-quality work …all apparently due to that much-used, misused, and abused condition called stress. But forget all that – how do YOU feel right now? Would you say life was a pain or a pleasure? If it is pleasure, are you masking the pain, drowning it in some substance, or perhaps inventing clever strategies to avoid it? If it is pain, (that is, stressful in any way), this book is definitely for you. If you don't have any mental or emotional discomfort, if you never ever see yourself as a victim, if you never point the finger of blame at others for how you feel, and if you think life is paradise, then this book is not for you. Please pass it on to someone else immediately!

Otherwise read on. There is much to learn, much to do and, most importantly, much to be!

But first – the myths. A number of dangerous myths have developed during the past three decades that have distorted our beliefs and are distracting attention away from the real reasons and cures of this apparently omnipresent ailment we call stress.

Are you sitting comfortably?

Myth 1

"Stress has a natural, positive part to play in modern life"

Not so!

There is no such thing as 'positive stress'. This term is an oxymoron! By definition, stress is unnatural and unhealthy, and therefore always a negative state. Here is the definition we will work with:

Stress is a form of pain that comes to tell you there is something you need to change. Pain – any pain – is a messenger saying there is something you need to learn.

While some people rightly differentiate pain from suffering where pain is physical and suffering is mental/emotional, I will, throughout the book use the term pain for both.

If you put your hand in the fire what do you experience? Pain. What do you learn? Not to do it again. You listened to the messenger, you learned, and you changed. We can experience stress or pain at four levels – spiritual, mental, emotional, and physical. When the messenger comes at the mental or emotional levels, with painful thoughts and negative feelings created by no-one but ourselves, do we listen to the messenger? No we don't, we either shoot the messenger or embrace it. Why? Because we have been taught to believe that some stress is necessary and good. 'They' told us it is normal, and we believed 'them'. And so we allow stress to develop within ourselves, not realizing we are creating our own demise. By saying that a little stress is OK

is to light the fuse of a slow-burning suicide mission. One reason why the developed world's health services are having such a tough time is because more and more of us are taking less and less responsibility for our own mental and emotional well-being. No one told us that a single negative thought could have a devastating effect on our immune system.

The second reason we don't listen to the messenger, learn, and change is that we have grown to like a 'shot' of fear, and a 'quick hit' of anger. Why? Because these emotions stimulate the production of certain addictive chemicals in our bodies. Many people cannot get through their day without their 'adrenaline fix'. So we go looking for bad situations, for confrontational people, for reasons to become angry, and if we don't get our fix then it feels like something is missing from our day.

To say that stress is normal, that a bit of stress is good, is a neat way of avoiding the inner work of self-responsibility and a sign of lazy thinking. We all learn to think lazily, it is largely an unfortunate consequence of our education (or lack of education), so most of us learn to believe that some stress is good. One thing is for sure, an increasing number of people are waking up to the reality that stress has no part in a fulfilling life and they are doing something about it at the level of their thoughts and feelings.

CAPPUCCINO CONVERSATIONS

Have you ever overheard a "Boy, it's tough out there" conversation? The first person starts with something like, "I tell you, I have so much to do, the deadlines are horrendous, my desk is piled high and everyone wants something from me yesterday, I'm so stressed out I could die!" Following the briefest of pauses the other person says, "You're stressed out! You should see what I have to do!" The next few minutes are a litany of "stuff" with each person struggling to prove that they are more stressed than their cappuccino companion. How crazy can we get, what kind of world have we created, are we creating, when we compete with each other to be more stressed? What kind of world measures success by levels of stress? You never do that, do you?

Myth 2

2

"You have to be a doctor to diagnose and treat stress"

No you don't!

Doctors only treat the physical symptoms, not the cause. Only you know the thoughts and feelings that lie at the root of your stress, and only you can change your thoughts, emotions, and feelings. No-one else creates your thoughts and feelings, and they don't just happen, though it feels that way sometimes. When you learn to identify and assess the quality of your thoughts and feelings you can begin to choose the ones you know are positive.

What are you thinking now? What are you feeling right now? And what is the quality of each? How often do you ask yourself these three questions? Probably seldom, usually never – it's just not part of our education. If we don't ask questions like, "What am I feeling and why am I thinking and feeling this way?" we may never get to know ourselves, we may never become truly self aware, and we will never know what it is like to consciously choose our own thoughts or feelings.

Some people say these kinds of introspective questions are the beginning of naval gazing or narcissism. But they are not. A few minutes every day in such a gentle inner enquiry, and you can learn to feel the pulse of your own feelings, and very quickly know more intimately than ever what you need to do to calm yourself and concentrate your energies in the most effective way.

Of course, if you have some serious physical discomfort then perhaps it's time for a visit to the doctor. But unless you change your thoughts and feelings the pain won't go away forever. Pills and potions are irrelevant to the task of putting positive power into what you think and feel. So perhaps it's time to be your own doctor, take your own pulse, feel your own feelings, and diagnose your own state of being. Only then will you be naturally interested in the "inner" remedies, treatments, and methods to help free yourself of the pain we call stress, and only then will you return to optimum mental and emotional health.

The treatments for your head and heart are a lot different to those for your body. When you truly, deeply realize that all your stress begins with your own thoughts and emotions, and that you are the only one responsible, only then will meditation, visualization, and positive thinking suddenly arouse your curiosity.

DECIBELS OF THOUGHT

Most of us think far too much – somewhere around 50,000 thoughts a day on average, so they say! Why is that too much? Because most of our thoughts are based on insecurity and worry about uncertain futures. In fact, most thinking is really worry camouflaged as care, anxiety disguised as concern. Thinking does not give us the strength we need to live a calmer, more fulfilling life. It drains our energy and obscures the access we need to our own inner wisdom. Thinking can easily be an inner noise that drowns out the voice of our heart. When we say, "I just need to think about that", we really mean "I'm not sure", which means there is doubt, and doubt is one of those habits which turns into worry and anxiety, and all they do is subtly drain our energy.

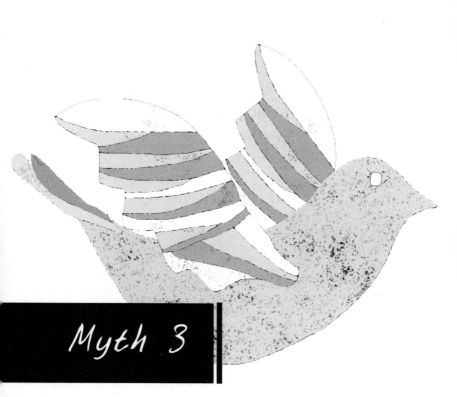

Myth 3

3

"Stress is necessary to achieve peak performance"

Definitely not!

It is a false belief that stress, or putting pressure on people, is necessary to get things done. Why? Because fear is being invoked and used as a motivator, and that always results in a drainage of energy, which eventually can lead to physical disease. Stressful thinking is fearful and angry thinking, and if sustained, leads to illness, absenteeism, poor performance, and the breakdown of relationships. The psychosomatic effects are well known. Tense thoughts lead to tight muscles and headaches, worried thoughts upset the digestion and can eventually result in an ulcer, fearful thinking speeds up and wears down the heart, inducing the over production of adrenaline, while anger has been identified as one of the major contributory factors in cancer.

Stress and fear, and therefore adrenaline, may appear to get things done fast and efficiently in the short-term – but in the long term it all leads to burnout. This is why there is no such thing as positive stress. Like those who have learned to believe stress is natural, those who advocate that stress is necessary to reach peak performance are also demonstrating lazy thinking, or the avoidance of doing the inner work of self-change. They are probably adrenaline junkies. And for those who still believe that the fight/flight response to people and situations is built into our psyche, dating back to Neanderthal man, and is therefore a natural response, perhaps it's time to think again!

Nothing is built in, everything is learned. Yes, you can fight or flee, but you could also choose from many other options. You can stand still, you can just smile, you can lie down, you can sing, you can dance! The reason we sometimes cannot see the other options when faced with a challenging situation is because our deepest learned habit is to create fear and then react from that fear, and it's fear that shuts down our ability to create choices, not to mention paralysing our ability to assess the strengths and weakness of each option and make the right choice.

We have been taught to believe that the fear is normal and natural – the narrowing of focus to concentrate on the threat. But the truth is that the fear paralyses our ability to create what may be much more appropriate and effective responses. Fear is a learned habit and very soon we are generating fearfulness at the slightest perceived threat. Contrary to popular belief fear has absolutely no value to our well-being. You don't even need fear to respond effectively to the unexpected encounter with a tiger. You need the cool, calm, and concentrated focus of the gymnast and the creativity of the artist to respond effectively. It's not the tiger that scares you, it's what you do with the tiger in your mind that generates the fear. Who or what are the tigers in your life? What are you doing with them in your mind?

So banish the belief that stress is necessary. Replace it with the understanding that stress kills, diminishes, drains, disempowers. Unlearn the habit of fearing and then use the workshop of life to practice choosing and enacting different responses to the deadline, the boss, the multitude of tasks, the difficult person in your life, the harsh tackle on the field of play – all those things which triggered your pain yesterday. They are your teachers today. They are opportunities to affirm your calm and creativity. They come to test both your capacity to choose the right response and your power to practice that response. If you don't start to be more creative and choose your responses you will suffer from the most common disease currently known to human kind. It's called victimitis! But you never play the victim…do you?

POWER OF GENIUS

The universe is made up of energy. Most of it is totally invisible. The physical visible energy is the weakest form that energy can take. One atom bomb may be powerful but it does not have "creative genius" within it. You do. You are a conscious creative being with the potential not only for genius but to influence the world. It's up to you. Any stress you are experiencing means you are not influencing anything but you are allowing the world to influence you. To find your inner power, to cultivate your genius, practice calm. When you understand that a peaceful mind is a creative mind you will realize that inner peace is also your personal power.

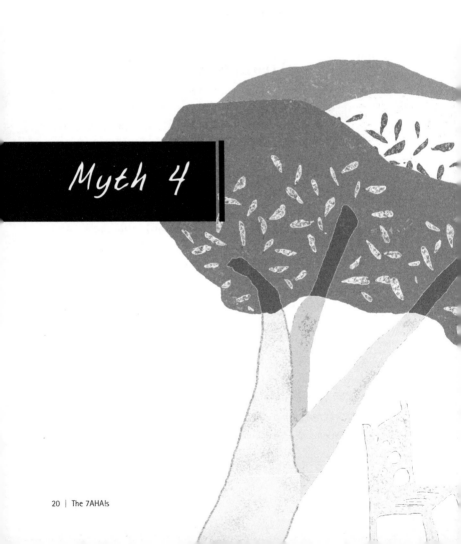

Myth 4

"Stress is simply a physical phenomena and some rest and relaxation will make it go away"

Absolute nonsense!

The root cause of all stress can be found in the non-physical realm of thoughts and feelings. Physical treatments, therapies, and relaxation strategies may relieve some symptoms, but they cannot change the way you think. Your thinking is the cause. And behind your thoughts your beliefs are a deeper cause.

The reason this myth has so much power in the world is that we think we are only physical forms, and that if we relax our bodies, our minds will follow. But it actually happens the other way round – by relaxing the mind the body follows suit. That's not to say we don't need to look after our bodies, we do, the body is our temple, our vehicle, our costume. Without it we would not be able to talk to each other and create our life experience. So perhaps it's time to wise up and cut down on the consumptions and activities that are aimed at the goal of relaxation. Pay much more attention to your thoughts and feelings, learn to manage them, learn to fill them with peace and calm, and then watch your personality change for the better as you restore your mental and then physical well-being. Everyone knows this intuitively. But still we get sucked in by the articles and the adverts which say, "Do this, consume that, go there, and you will be stress-free". Nonsense. If it were true, the levels of stress in life, in general, would be going down, not up. We now buy and consume more things, travel to more places, and create more sophisticated forms of entertainment, all in the name of relaxation, than ever before. And yet, almost every day there seems to be new set of statistics saying levels of stress, anxiety, insecurity, and work-place pressures are on the rise.

Watch yourself when you get home tonight. Into the lounge you go, can or cup in hand, straight to the couch, reaching for the remote, and on comes the flickering screen. The midnight movie is Rambo III – ninety minutes of stress, terror, fear, anger, frustration, etc. And we call this relaxation. See how clever the marketing men are. They have convinced us that stimulation is relaxation. Perhaps it's time to awaken from this pervasive illusion!

NEW AGE OR OLD AGE

Never believe anyone who says you cannot change, or that you should not tamper with your personality. The truth is, you are already changing numerous times every day. And it is never too late to contemplate a change in personality, which simply means changing the way you see and respond to people and the world around you. It is up to you. You can either live with the pain that is known as stress - it's what most people do because it seems the easiest way to live - or you set off on the adventure of self-discovery. This is not some New Age fad. Every time you change one of your old habits of creating pain as a response to life, it will be one more step towards enjoying a riper old age. If you want to live a long and healthy life, kill your stress and your pain with truth, before it kills you!

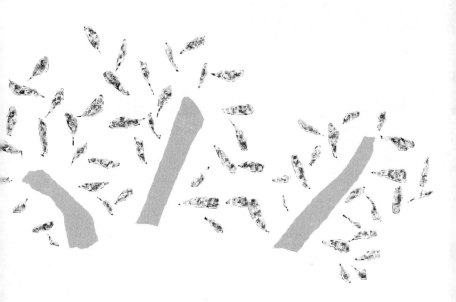

Myth 5

"A change of diet, a little jogging, and a good holiday will banish stress"

Sorry, simply not true!

For the same reason as the previous myth, diets, running, and vacations may relieve some of the symptoms temporarily, but they will not provide a cure. That's not to say a healthy diet and exercise are not important, they are, but they will not free you from stress. You may remember the jogging craze of the eighties. Every local park was motorways for thousands of track-suited runners, faces lined in pain, sweat pouring out of breathless bodies, all in the name of balance and relaxation. And relaxation was achieved, because after two miles they were absolutely exhausted. Relaxation is not exhaustion or fatigue. Relaxation is the ability to relax your mind anywhere, anytime, and know that your body will follow.

Going on holiday in the 21st century may still be an adventure; it is still a change of scene, people, food, and climate. And change can still (sometimes) be as good as a rest. But now you know that you don't need to go anywhere to rest, relax your mind, and replenish your heart. Now you know that wherever you go you will still be with yourself when you arrive. And what you think, feel, and do there is likely to be exactly what you think, feel, and do wherever you are now.

But you may be thinking, "What about the fun of the party, the healthiness of playing sport, or the comfort of the sofa when there's no work to think about?" To an enlightened soul real happiness cannot be found at a good party. Parties, like running, like watching TV, like chasing a little ball around the court, are ways of avoiding the inner work of self-control and self-mastery. Keep enjoying your leisure activities, don't

stop exercising, don't stop going to parties, just don't expect any of them to free you from your stress, or give you a real and lasting feeling of happiness. They may provide relief from some of the pain, a temporary high that feels like happiness, but it's an illusory happiness. Perhaps you sense the truth of this already.

It's probably not what you wanted to hear, and you may now be thinking, "I just don't agree". And that's fine. But think about your reason for disagreeing. Is it because your partying and running are under threat, or is it because you haven't thought it through deeply? Why do you think that after so many remedies for stress have been invented, written about, manufactured, marketed, and consumed, there is more stress out there than ever before? Simple − it's called avoidance. We avoid doing the inner work of taking responsibility for our own thoughts and feelings. Everything in our life, including our destiny, begins in our own head. I'm sorry to keep repeating this, but it took me so long to really "get it" I had to hear it a hundred times in a hundred different ways.

RETREAT YOUR SELF!

Holidays come from the idea of holy day – a day that is sacred and devoted to rest and renewal. Not for bingeing and whinging, not for sleeping and slothing! Holidays are whole days devoted to the self, so that we may find and be replenished by the peace of spirit – the peace that already exists, and always has existed, in our own hearts. It is a time to recharge our spiritual batteries from inside out, and to remind us of our true purpose in life. Are you aware of your own inner peace of spirit and do you know your true purpose in life? Very few do! Hot tip – set aside at least two holy days each year and take yourself on a spiritual retreat. Not a religious retreat, a spiritual retreat! There is a difference.

Myth 6

"You have to be working 14 hours a day and constantly under pressure to experience stress"

No you don't!

Some people only work a few hours a day, and are hardly ever confronted by deadlines or other pressures, but they are more stressed than those working long hours to tight deadlines. It's not what you do, or when you have to do it by, that causes your stress; it's how you perceive the "whats" and "whens" of daily life that generates your stress. It's your perception.

Have you ever watched two people doing the same or similar work, to the same deadlines? One tears their hair out with almost palpable anxiety. For the other, it's a breeze. Why the difference? Perception. It's how each one perceives what they do, and the possible outcome. Your perception is based on your beliefs. If you believe that

your happiness is based on what you do, and that people get fired for missing a deadline, or that authority figures in your life have a right to punish you, and cause you pain for non-completion, then stress will be your companion wherever you go, whatever you do, for the rest of your life. But if you believe in yourself, if you

believe you can control your emotions, if you believe that no one can hurt you without your permission, if you believe that missing a deadline is not the end of the world, or your job, or that some deadlines will always be missed in life and that does not diminish you as a person, then you will always be able to relax, no matter where you are, or how tight the deadline. And, paradoxically, you will be much less likely to miss the deadline than the habitual worrier.

Are you ready to challenge your beliefs? It's not other people, or the system, or the hand life seems to deal you that keep you locked in stressful patterns of thought and behavior. It's your beliefs. Change your beliefs and you change everything.

Beliefs don't come built into your DNA. All beliefs are learned. We learn them and send them into our subconscious, and they then pop up and out through our thoughts, emotions, and words. The problem is we not only hold beliefs, we identify with them, and some of us will even kill and die for them. This is extremely silly when you realize that belief is not the truth, and nothing is worth dying for. But you may believe differently. And that's just fine by me as I am not here to convince you of anything. In fact, you must not believe a word I say!

A LIFE OF TIME IS A LIFETIME.

The clock on the wall is not time, it is simply a way of symbolizing the passage of human experience. It is not our master, it is our creation. You cannot save time, lose time, or rush time. Well, you can actually, in a way, because you ARE time. Time is life and you are life. When you spend time you spend yourself. So be careful how you spend yourself. Don't let anyone else spend your life. Consult the wise on how they have spent their lives. You cannot lose time but you can waste time. You cannot save time but you can save lives. Start with your own. It begins simply, with awareness, self-awareness. Wisdom will follow naturally.

Myth 7

7

"Other people, situations, and events are responsible for your stress"

No, they're not!

This is the most common myth, otherwise known as the global disease called "victimitis, as mentioned earlier. The way we respond to people and events lies at the heart of our stress. Stress-management is really self-management. To take someone to court because you think they caused your stress sustains the illusion that you are not responsible for what you think, feel, decide and do. In other words, you are saying that someone else can live your life for you.

This is by far the commonest myth or illusion because our whole world tends to operate on the premise that others are responsible for how we feel and what happens in our life. Even the leaders of nations blame others for what they feel, and thereby demonstrate how they disempower themselves, and play the victim. Listen to your conversations with others and count how many times and the different ways that you find to say, "I am the victim", or "I feel like this because of someone or something else".

True stress management or self management is based on the principle of taking total responsibility for any and every feeling of emotional /mental /spiritual discomfort. True stress management or self management is choosing to respond proactively to whatever is happening outside

our self. It's not the late train or the scratched car that causes you to be upset, it is how you choose to respond to those events. If your response is stressful it is a sign that you are dependent on your car for your self-worth, or the approval of others for your self-esteem. These basic mistakes are learned early in life and can lock us in pain for our entire lives if we let them. Never base your self-esteem or self-worth on anything external.

Taking responsibility for your ability to respond, choosing to maintain your calm and composure, ensuring you remain positive in the face of all and every kind of event, is the sign of an enlightened soul in a very unenlightened world. But to cultivate these abilities means it's time to be a student again. To reach the stage where we can remain cool and calm when all around us choose panic and chaos means we need to be prepared to learn about our inner self, to learn how to control our thinking, to learn to challenge our beliefs, and to choose different perceptions. Once you see that it's you who hurts yourself, not the other person who hurts you, you are half way home. The other half of the journey is breaking the habit of blaming and projecting your pain on to others.

The other person is never the problem! When you truly see this you will be awake and free again.

LOOK, LISTEN, AND LOVE

Don't forget that everyone is always in two places at once – they are "out there" but they are also "in here", in your head. If you get angry with them out there, you are not only the first to suffer, you are in effect getting angry with yourself. And that is like taking a knife and sticking it in your own body. You wouldn't choose to do that would you? Never ever get angry. And if you do, and you will, until you have learned to kick the habit, don't get angry with yourself for getting angry. Heal the anger with wisdom and love from your own heart, for yourself. It's there. All you have to do is stop, look inward, and listen. Ask someone who is already doing it to explain how. Better still – learn how to meditate. That's what meditation is for.

Section Two

Wisdom and Truth

The Seven Essential Insights into Your Self

The Need to Know!

You can spend your life driving a car and never know what's wrong when it breaks down. You are then completely at the mercy of others to fix it. At that moment you probably think to yourself, "God, I wish I knew how this thing works..." Sound familiar? Unfortunately, God cannot help with car mechanics!

It's almost the same with your SELF. If you don't know who you are, and how you work, how can you work out how to fix things when they break down? As we have seen, the presence of any stress, or any form of mental/emotional pain, is a signal that something has broken down inside the engine of your consciousness. We are not talking about the body here. If you have something seriously wrong with your body you obviously need to see a doctor. But even then, if you are a little enlightened, you know that the original cause of your physical disease lies within your consciousness, your state of mind, your feelings and emotions, which, in turn, lies in your beliefs, most of which lie deep down in your subconscious. So, if repairs are to be carried out you need to know certain things – essential things – about your spirit, mind, heart, and body.

If we are to manage our self and our life successfully, it pays us to go back to school. Not the school of our childhood and not to learn the 3Rs, but to learn about ourselves – the one subject that was missing in all our educations. Are you ready to go back to school? Are you humble enough to put on the hat of the student and be a learner again? Are you interested enough to learn about the mechanisms of your own consciousness, which create the outcomes of your life? If you are interested and you do value continuous learning you will find that real learning has nothing to do with having to remember things, in fact, it is more like the opposite. The real lessons of life do not need to be remembered because they cannot be forgotten. That's what makes real learning a joyful, awakening, empowering experience. When you do put on your learning hat again you will see that your life is your school, every scene is a workshop, your teachers are all around you, and every interaction carries a potential lesson to be discerned and learned.

There are probably seven million things you could know about yourself that would be useful, but not all would be immediately necessary. But there are seven things that are immediately useful, and probably essential, to your well-being right now. Any one of them will help you understand how and why you create pain for yourself, and how to can fix things yourself, without needing to go and see someone with an "ist" at the end of their job title!

JUST IN CASE

Some people don't know how to identify pain. They have been in pain for so long they have come to think of it as normal, even beneficial. Some even become addicted to their pain. All of the following emotions are different forms of pain, and each one is telling us there is something we need to learn in order to make changes in the way we create our life experience: anger, irritation, frustration, rage, anxiety, tension, fear, terror, sadness, melancholy, depression, hopelessness, powerlessness, worry. Our belief systems have taught us that they are a natural part of life, but they are not. They require healing. We also need to know how not to create them in the first place.

Insight 1

Your Identity

You are not what you have been taught to think you are!

This is the deepest, most profound and most important insight, but it will have little value or power if you treat it as a quick read. Read it 20 times a day, dwell on it, contemplate it, challenge it, and meditate on it. Realize the reality of it within your self. This one insight will, if you allow it, transform your life. Are you ready? Are you sitting comfortably? Then let yourself begin.

What you see in the bathroom mirror in the morning is not you – it's only your body. The moment you think (believe) you are your body you automatically think (believe) you will grow old and ugly and die. Though your body will, YOU don't. But if you believe that YOU do, you will think according to that belief, and you will give birth to fear. And, as we saw earlier, all forms of stress have their roots in fear.

All fear has its roots in the fear of death, fear of loss, or fear of the ending of comfort. They are all forms of death and this is why 99.99 per cent of all people experience some stress (fear) every day: because we have all been taught to believe we are only physical entities. However, belief is seldom truth, and in this case we need the truth to set us free of false belief! In this case the truth will set you free of fear, and therefore stress.

The truth is that you are not that body you see reflected in the mirror: you are a soul, you are spirit. It is not that you have a soul or spirit somewhere in your body, you ARE a soul. You are it! You, the soul, are conscious and self-aware. Soul, self, spirit, and consciousness are synonymous. You are not the body you occupy. The body is the dwelling and you are the dweller. You animate the body. It is your car, your temple. You cannot be cut, burned, drowned, or set on fire. Your body can, but YOU cannot.

Scientists have nothing to say about soul, because the soul cannot be captured in a test tube. That's why you must not believe a word of what you read or hear (including here!) – you must put it to the test. Only when you test this insight, and experience it to be a reality, will it be true for you. Belief is not truth, and the greatest truth is your own experience, or in this case 'insperience' because, in order to 'insperience' as you truly are you must withdraw your attention from the world 'out there' and transfer it to the world within. Do this only for a few minutes to begin with, until you are accustomed to the method. The following is the method.

Think of yourself as a conscious, self-aware, point of spiritual light sitting inside your head just above and behind the eyes. Your body is simply your car, your temple, your costume. Meditate on this insight and gradually it will become a direct 'insperience'. You will begin to go beyond your own thoughts (you are not your thoughts) and into the direct experience of your silent self. You will begin to realize and experience yourself as non-physical, therefore not subject to death, and therefore eternal, and therefore without the need to fear anything. As this truth becomes more real in everyday situations you will begin to feel less fearful, less unsure, less anxious, less helpless, less dependent, and less powerless. Slowly but surely, in every area of your life, you will begin to feel calmer, more relaxed, and more confident in your power and ability to handle the challenges which you encounter in everyday life.

Now, the truth is, you already knew all this, you just forgot. So the trick is to remind yourself a hundred times a day – you are not your name, position, nationality, or belief system. They are labels and roles, but they are not you. You are not even male or female. You are the being aspect of the human, the mind not the matter, the soul not the body. You are not even your thoughts and feelings. When you realize this, then change will come easily, all your problems will begin to dissolve, and a natural happiness and a deep inner peace will return.

DYING ALIVE

There is an old Buddhist saying – "If you die before you die, then when you die, you don't die". This simply means that when you cease to identify with anything that is not the essential you, then you are, in a sense, dead. It means that you have chosen to die to illusion, the illusion that you are physical, the illusion that you are your nationality, profession, possessions, etc., and you are now fully alive, aware, and alert to reality of who you are. This is why the art of detachment is such a powerful way to inner freedom and peace.

Insight 2

Your Nature

You are drop-dead stunningly gorgeous, but you won't see your beauty in the bathroom mirror!

It doesn't really matter if you think you are good-looking or not. Real beauty cannot be touched, or even seen with physical eyes. You will see and touch true beauty when you feel your own inner peace. You will know and feel real beauty when you can give away anything with love and not want anything in return. You will experience your real beauty when you are content with yourself and your life inside, without any stimulation from outside. For these are the true experiences and expressions of beauty that come from inside out.

Our real nature is not anger and hate, fear or sadness – these are all learned and created on our journey through life as we become influenced by others and the world around us. When you accept this possibility, experiment with it in meditation, and directly 'insperience' these inner qualities of your true core self, you will realize that inner peace, true love (not romantic love), and real happiness are all non-dependent. You are a beautiful and powerful soul, you always have been, you just forgot. You lost awareness of your true self; you lost sight of your inner beauty. You believed others as they made comments about your body, "Ah look, isn't he a big handsome boy" or "Doesn't she have a gorgeous figure?" And in these moments you believed you are your body, and you fell under the spell of the illusion that beauty was only physical. In those moments you fatally learned to build your self-esteem on how you look.

You also lost awareness of your true self and your real beauty when people started to make comments about your personality and behaviors. The moment you found that telling jokes drew attention, or being shy drew sympathy, or being aggressive invoked fear in others, you began to create your self-image around certain negative behaviors.

Give yourself a break. Give yourself a chance to remember, to "insperience" and to realize who you really are, and you will rediscover your true nature, which is peaceful, loving, contented, and very powerful. These are the inner treasures of every human being, regardless of what they think, believe, do, or have done. These attributes are the true nature or natural qualities of the self, and that means every self! They are qualities for which every human being is always searching, and they cannot be found at the local store. They don't come in boxes or bottles. They come from inside out. They are states of being which can be accessed within you at any moment. You only need to be a little curious, and prepared to give them your attention. Like small, shy children they need you to look in towards them, love them a little, and coax them out of your own heart. If you do, you will discover real wealth, the wealth of your true, underlying, eternal, gorgeous nature.

As soon as you give expression to any of these treasures, as soon as you bring peace to a loud and aggressive meeting, as soon as you offer acceptance and forgiveness where others expect judgment and punishment, as soon as you are content with what you have and show others how to be the same, you are giving expression to your natural beauty. You are giving the gifts of your self to others. And guess what will come back? Perhaps not immediately, but eventually, the same must return.

FATAL IDENTITY

Look at the football fanatic and feel compassion. He has lost himself in his team, the colors, the badge, the club, and his heroes. He knows not who he really is, and he is under the illusion he is a football fan, and because of that he knows not what he does. He knows and yet ...he doesn't. The moment you identify with anything that is not you – an object, an idea, a philosophy, a team ...whatever...you are lost in the illusion of what you are not, and that is how you invite fear and anger to be your companions and take up residence within your character. Your beauty is lost to the world and your heart sheds its own tears and mourns that loss every day.

Insight 3

Your Responsibility

Your destiny never leaves your hands. It only seems to!

The moment you point your physical or mental finger at anyone or anything to blame them for how you feel, you give your power away. No one and no thing can make you feel anything without your permission. Or to put it another way: It's not what you say or do to me that makes me feel this way, it's what I do with what you do or say to me that makes me feel this way. That line is worth reading ten times until you memorize it. It is a gateway to true freedom and the restoration of your personal power.

Ultimately, the responsibility for how you respond to life around you, and therefore what comes back to you, lies in the choice of your perception. Your perception is your interpretation of what is happening around you and yes, it is a choice, but only if you are self-aware enough to make it.

Your perception will totally influence what you think, feel, and do in response to the people and the world around you. If you perceive someone in a negative way then you will respond with negative energy and you will be the first to suffer. You will send them a small package of highly invisible negative energy, which will one day come right back to the sender.

Most of us are trained, conditioned, even brainwashed by our parents and society to perceive the negative, and see the worst in a person or situation, even in ourselves. It's no wonder there is so much unhappiness around, especially in so-called developed societies where most people are living in relative comfort. The habit of perceiving the negative and taking a pessimistic view is now pervasive in our world. No matter how well things are going, a negatively conditioned mind (belief system) will always perceive the negative,

look for the negative and even invent the negative when it's not there. Sometimes the media is quite brilliant at this dark art! It then spreads like a contagious disease.

The ultimate perception is that everything that happens, and that means everything, happens for a reason. Hidden in everything that happens around you and to you there is a meaning, a lesson, an insight to be perceived, to be seen, and felt. But if you take things personally, and perceive things wrongly, you will not see the underlying meaning of events or the significance of the presence of certain people, and you may easily miss the lessons of life. You will react automatically instead of responding creatively. Your emotions will control you instead of you deciding exactly what you feel. This both feels and looks like slavery. The moment you attribute what you feel, think, and do to someone else you are, in that moment, making yourself their personal slave.

Self-mastery is being aware of our perception and consequent thoughts, consciously choosing both and then acting accordingly. The outcome, or the result, is known as destiny. Look at your outcomes so far – your 'outer' outcomes (where you are, what you are doing, the state of your relationships) and your 'inner' outcomes (your state of being, level of self-esteem, etc.). Are there any outcomes you would like to change? Yes? Then don't be daft enough to try to change events or other people (which is what most people try to do). Events that we would like to change are always in the past, and both people and the past are the two things in life you can never, ever change. Next time, choose to change your response, beginning with your perception. When you do change your perception and therefore your response, only then will you find that your destiny is back in your own hands. The only thing you are fully responsible for in this lifetime is your own destiny. Don't give it to someone else.

WAKING PERCEPTION

They say perception is reality, and it is, for each and every one of us. Is the glass half full or half empty; are you a nasty, miserable, pessimistic, unhappy, and self-centred being…a "looking after a number one" kind of person? Or are you a generous, unlimited, caring, selfless, positive, unconditionally loving kind of person? However you choose to perceive yourself, then so you will be. And so you will act, and so will be your destiny. Your perception is both your reality and your choice. If you can learn to make this choice you will be an awakened soul and enlightenment will come easily.

Insight 4

Your Beliefs

Forget blind faith, it's blind belief that makes life an unhappy, stressful experience.

The most powerful influences on your life, from day one to the final moments, are invisible, intangible, and buried deep down inside your consciousness.

There are at least hundreds, probably thousands, of beliefs within your subconscious. They are outside your day-to-day, moment-to-moment awareness, until you say in an argument or debate, "I believe..." Beliefs can be likened to a computer program. They have been collected, absorbed, assimilated, and learned during your whole life, and there are traces from previous lives. They are the most powerful influence on your perception of yourself and the world around you.

The most common beliefs about the self begin with the words "I can't". And if you believe you can't, then guess what, you won't! Your destiny will be partly but significantly decided in that moment. Or if you believe you are unworthy of happiness, for whatever reason, then guess what, you will never be happy. It is as simple as that. Such beliefs about your self are known as "fatal beliefs". They are fatal because they stop you expanding your capacity; they stop you stepping outside your comfort zones. They stop you learning, changing, growing, and being all that you can be. So they really are fatal.

In our relationships we tend to create "blocker beliefs". The moment you judge and fix a label on someone you block the flow of energy in that relationship. It is so easy to do and it shows up in how you talk about others, for example, "The boss is stupid...my boy is crazy...the President is a nasty person." In these moments of judgment and condemnation we cease to try to understand the other and the relationship is effectively paralysed. Be careful what you think and say about others.

To expand the picture slightly; if you believe in evolution then you believe that life is a survival course where only the strongest endure, and you will therefore perceive the world to be a dangerous and threatening place, full of winners and losers. You will think competitively and your predominant emotion will be fear in its many forms. You will try to manipulate and control others in order to survive. You will become extremely upset when you experience failure, which you surely must. And you will be doomed to a life of stress (fear), failure (you simply cannot control another human being) and, as a consequence, low self-esteem. This is the power and effect of just one belief in your life.

If you explore, examine, question, and challenge your beliefs, you will quickly come to see that one belief is responsible for all the pain and suffering in the world. It is the belief that we are physical, limited, and mortal beings whose beauty and therefore success and happiness are dependent on our shape, appearance, and whatever material items can be accumulated. It is the core wrong belief and the greatest mistake ever made. We all inherit this belief, which gets stronger with every passing generation. So we all learn to make the same mistake. Look at this belief, think about it, and the moment you realize it's an illusion you will be a hair's breadth away from the truth. And remember, the reward of truth is freedom. And true happiness is the reward of real freedom.

TO TRUST OR NOT TO...

In the context of our relationships we all believe the following about at least one other person: "They cannot be trusted". In so many of our relationships, trust seems to be the first thing to go and the last to come back. Why? Because somebody did something yesterday, or last week, which let us down, and we felt hurt, we felt pain. And we attributed our pain to them. We believed they hurt us. Sorry. This is wrong. Please repeat the following a hundred times a day, "No one can hurt me, but I can use others to hurt myself". Or, put another way, no one can hurt you without your permission. Remember school? Sing after me...sticks and stones will break my bones...To think someone can hurt you is an extremely common belief, but extremely unenlightened.

Insight 5

Self Control

You think you're free, don't you? No you're not! Not until you make conscious daily choices about what you do with the energy of your life.

Do you have control over your life? Or do you spend much of your time trying to control others? If you do the latter you are doomed to failure. If there is one thing you cannot control in life, it is other human beings. But the most common human behavior in all corners of the world is trying to control others – physically, emotionally, or mentally.

The moment you become the slightest bit upset with anyone it means you are trying to control what you cannot control. You are also likely to be aping the behavior of parents, teachers, or any of those 'big people' we all watched when we were young.

This was where you learned to try to control what you cannot control. If you use a threat to cajole someone into doing something, and they do it, you may fall under the illusion that you are controlling them, but it is most certainly an illusion. They still control their thoughts and decisions, but it's as if they lose awareness of that, and it is as if they are motivated by fear, which you seem to have created in them. But it wasn't you, it was they who created that fear. In the same way, you attribute your fear to others when you have created it yourself. The day will come when you meet someone who will not respond to your threat. They have realized that they are responsible for their own emotional reactions regardless of who is in front of them, and they have become assertive enough not to let themselves be bullied emotionally.

On the other side of this coin, perhaps you think that others are controlling you – they are not. The worst, most dictatorial government in the world does not control the people without their permission! Perhaps there are one or two people in your personal life that you always seem to bow down or submit to. That simply means you need to work on your self-image, self-belief, and self-esteem (they are all connected). No-one can control you...full stop. You do not 'have to' think, feel, or do anything. You don't even have to get up and go to work in the morning. But you probably think you do 'have to', because you believe you do, and you believe everyone else has to as well. Why? Because you think (believe) that society is controlling you. It isn't.

Taking control of your own life means waking up to the illusions you have assimilated from your family, education, and culture. Hacking through the jungle of false beliefs and getting to the truth means taking time to listen to the wisdom of the ages outside, and working with it on the inside. It means challenging every belief, not resisting, arguing, or fighting, but challenging your beliefs, simply because both your head and your heart want to know the truth. But you are too busy for all that...aren't you? Is that what you say, "Sorry, I'm just too busy for this introspective stuff!" All you are saying is that you value doing something else more than you value waking up! It's always a personal choice. But we prefer to think of ourselves as victims of the organization, the government, even the past, rather than take control of our own lives. Being a victim is easier, especially when everyone else is doing it, too. Being a victim is living in self-created suffering.

If you do decide to awaken then you will find you can control your self, your thoughts, feelings, and behaviors and therefore your life. And when you do, your happiness, your peace of mind, and your personal power will always only be a second away. Unfortunately, many prefer to stay asleep and blame the world for their pain.

NO PROBLEM!

When you understand that ultimately there is no such thing as a problem, only situations that can be improved, you are effectively choosing to hold the most proactive perception. There is room for improvement in every situation because there is room for improvement in every one of us. Unfortunately, we use the language of problems to describe almost all situations, events, and circumstances, including those within our own minds and hearts, and the moment we do our energy dissipates. And then we find it hard to understand why the situation or event happened in the first place. We need to know the cause in order to know the cure. Ultimately, an enlightened soul knows that a problem is just a perception. It is only one interpretation of a situation. More positive and self-empowering perceptions include challenge, opportunity, and lesson. These enlightened perceptions then give rise to a much more creative response. The truth is that all problems exist only in the mind. The day you truly see the truth of that you will know you have just had a definite AHA! moment!

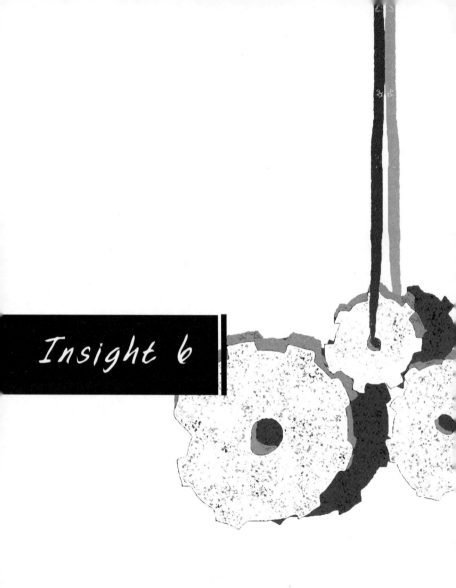

Insight 6

Life's Paradoxes

You are already perfect, you already have all that you will ever need, and you are already completely free, you just don't know it.

Life is filled with paradox. For example, if you want to be comfortable you have to let go of your comforts. Attachment to anything that you think brings you comfort is what makes you feel uncomfortable. You won't realize this, until you learn that real comfort, the comfort of your heart, does not come from objects, people, or anything external. True comfort, true relaxation, is a state of being that is created inside, not outside.

Another paradox is that in order to receive you have to give. Not a new idea, but very few people truly live it. If you want love and respect you have to give love but not expect anything in return. In other words, not want it! Confusing isn't it? If you keep loving and respecting you will soon realize that you are the first to receive the love and respect that you give, simply because you feel it first on its way out! When you know and live by the truth that what you give is what you get, and when you experience what you need in the very act of giving it, this sets you free of neediness and wanting. Ultimately, you may arrive beyond the duality of giving and receiving and realize that 'being' is both giving and receiving. When you have self-respect, when your being is filled with self-respect, then you are both giving and receiving respect at the same time.

This also opens the gates to what could be the greatest paradox, which is that you already are, and always have

been, perfectly beautiful, happy, and content. It's just that you are not aware of it. This is sometimes referred to as 'already always'. It's been a long journey, during which you have gathered many memories, impressions, false beliefs, misperceptions. All of these are like the layers of an onion and they cover the pure, powerful, and peaceful core of your own being – the perfect you – just as you were created. Which makes all self-development, as we know it, a little futile. You don't actually need to develop yourself to be the real you. You only have to become aware of everything that is false and then drop it. See 'the false' inside your consciousness - false beliefs, false under- standing, and false identities, and once you see them, falseness begins to drop away. And the final paradox? You won't see them by looking for them. The two most effective ways are through meditation and spending time with people who have already done it. Choose your company care- fully. The company you keep colors your consciousness, strengthening many of those layers which stop you from seeing and being your self.

In the context of our relationships we looked at the issue of control (page 57) and saw that we do not control others, but we do influence each other. As soon as you try to control someone, what do they do? They build a barrier, a wall – you're not getting through and they are not coming out to play. The result is that your capacity to influence diminishes. The more you try to control others, even if it's just in your own mind, the less influence you will have, whereas the less you try to control the more influence you will have. Try it. This is one of the key secrets of success in all relationships. But remember, the moment you want to influence you are in fact attempting to control. Pure influence has no motive. And that is enlightenment.

HAPPINESS IS ...

So what do you really want in life or out of life? Don't say you don't know...you do know! Be aware of why you do everything. What is your deepest motive? It is to experience happiness. Everything that you do is driven by the desire to be happy. What you have forgotten is that you are already happy. You do not need to look for it, work for it, strive for it, attempt to buy it, achieve your goals to experience it. All those things simply delay it. Happiness is already there within you. All you need to do is decide to be happy, and then make that decision a habit. Happiness is not a dependency, it is a decision. Come on, be happy! Even better...share your happiness. Begin with your heart. Wear a permanent smile on your heart and then make sure your heart is connected to your face. Then you will be happy faster, deeper, and longer! If happiness is not the right word replace it with contentment. Contentment is the happiness of spirit.

Insight 7

Your Relationships

Each and every one of us is a source of love, truth, peace, and contentment in the world. This is what makes us all naturally rich.

Life is relationship. Our lives are a series of relationships, whether they are with people, nature, objects, or God. Relationship is the giving and receiving of energy. And when the energy of the exchange carries benevolence, good wishes, or is simply positive in quality, then our relationships are in harmony. But that is not what we are taught. We are not taught to give and receive, but to take and keep; to take what you can and to keep what you can get. And because of these two habits alone we kill the harmony of our relationships at an individual and collective level.

But everybody is doing it, so it seems the right thing to do, until one day we awaken to the truth that everything is for giving, and it is not possible to possess anything. In that moment there is the return of harmony within ourselves, but perhaps not within others, as they continue with their illusion that we are here to accumulate and own, take and keep.

Enlightened souls know the age-old law, what goes around, comes around. What is sown is reaped. It is the principle of karmic returns. The enlightened soul knows that real wealth does not arrive in our bank accounts; it is already in our conscious accounts, or our spiritual bank within. Most of us are not aware we even have an inner savings account, a source of wealth, at that level. And while most people demonstrate by their intentions and actions that they believe money is the highest and most important form of wealth, the enlightened soul knows the highest and most precious resource of energy is spiritual.

This energy takes many forms, and our relationships are precisely the opportunity to shape and give our richest resource to each other. Love, truth, peace, and happiness are the primary colors of the soul, the primary forms of the inner spiritual energy that we all are. And once discovered, all relationships are seen in their true light, as opportunities to creatively shape and share those energies in the most appropriate way. Acceptance, caring, appreciation, and forgiving are all forms of love. Wisdom and insight are forms of truth. Contentment, satisfaction, and fulfilment are forms of happiness. None of these states are meant for keeping, they are sustained only when they are generated, radiated, and emitted out into the world. Why else are you here?

The truly enlightened soul has an even deeper awareness. Two fascinating dynamics kick in when the bank account of spirit is open, and real giving begins. One, the giver is first to experience the energy on the way out (to give love is to experience love)…and two, not only does energy return (as it must, because it is the law) but it returns at different levels. Spiritual wealth shared one day becomes monetary wealth received the next day, but never when profit is sought.

And so this is relationship. When all the other games are stripped away, relationship is an opportunity to be creative, because we are all artists of life, our own life. We each have the opportunity to invite and be invited by each other to co-create our lives, using the highest, the deepest, and the greatest wealth: the wealth that is hidden within the self. Don't hide your treasures. Don't let the cynics suppress your treasure. Don't allow the 'negaholics' to dampen your spirit. Live well, laugh often, and love much. Expect absolutely nothing in return and then watch the universe rush to build a camp at your feet. Being abundant attracts abundance.

COMFORT LEVELS

Why is it we seem to be at ease with some people and at total dis-ease with others? We tend to think it's their personality, or perhaps their mannerisms, or their attitude, which keep us in an unrelaxed state. But it's not. It is something within us that is uneasy and they are only the trigger. Perhaps they remind us of a stressful relationship in the past, perhaps we are thinking and acting at a completely different rhythm. More likely they are reflecting something within us that we would rather not see and acknowledge. One thing is sure; our teachers are those in whose company we feel the greatest unease. But don't tell them that.

Section Three

Action and Transformation
The Seven AHA!s of Highly Enlightened Souls

Are You Ready to Make a Few Positive Changes?

If you recognized the myths, and you can see their presence inside your head, you will also notice they are the perpetrators of much of your mental and emotional discomfort. Then all you need to do is ask yourself if you are ready to make some inner changes, that only you can make, to yourself and therefore your life.

If you recognized the truths, or simply saw some wisdom in the insights into your essential self and how life works, then you are ready to begin your own journey of discovery – an adventure into self- awareness and self-realization, not in some holiday paradise, but within your own being.

If you can see the value and envisage the benefits of doing a little work on your self, of being more self-aware, of taking back your personal power, of learning how not to be a victim, then you will make a difference in this world – first to your own life experience, and then to the lives of others. There is nothing more certain than when you change one small habit, someone in your life will notice it, and in that moment they will be changed, too.

If you are ready to do a little 'inner work', to restore your spiritual power and begin to radiate into the world the subtle energies of the love and peace which already lie at the centre of your heart, then you will change the world. You will not know precisely what you changed, but you will know you have been instrumental in some way.

So let's get practical. What can you do to get started? The word 'do' is not totally accurate here, because the origins of all that you do can be found inside your consciousness, within your mind and intellect. This is known as your state of 'being'. We are human beings, not human doings. Everything we do springs from our state of being. Being is therefore the first action. And that's why this strategy for personal change is really a strategy towards reawakening our ability to choose and create our state of being. This is a process which is almost entirely internal, invisible, and incognito. It is a secret strategy because no one will know what you are doing inside – unless you tell them. Don't tell them! If you do, some are likely to laugh, scoff, and pour cold water over your intentions to empower yourself and to be yourself. If you are going to change the way you are now, if you are going to decide to choose and create your state of being, it is likely to be a threat to them, and they will try to keep you the same. Unless they too are a little enlightened, in which case they are your best friends at this time, people with whom you can compare notes, discuss, and explore the deeper issues of personal transformation and share the experiences of your inner journey.

The path to enlightenment is filled with many realizations and AHA! moments! Perhaps you've had a few already. However, it is only a highly enlightened soul who translates the AHA! moment into action in such way as to make it life and lifestyle changing.

Here are the seven AHA!s, which then become important conscious practices of the highly enlightened soul. If you 'see' and act on just one of these with any consistency it will change your life. You will change your life.

The 1st AHA!

Be Quiet

The greatest power is the power of silence, and the essential self is silent.

Have you ever wondered why libraries have special atmospheres? They are places where many congregate but where silence is the code. Quietness in an atmosphere means there is the presence of quiet minds, and quiet minds are not only relaxed, they can concentrate easily and create more freely. Imagine you are in the library of your mind, browsing the accumulated wisdom on the shelves of your life – listen to the silence, be aware of the stillness. Ask any of the inner voices that may come to interupt your attentiveness to please be quiet! A quiet mind permits you to listen to your heart. Now you can allow your creativity to blossom. Now you can allow thoughts, ideas, images, and insights to emerge from the shadows of your subconscious on to the radiant screen of your mind. Now you can choose what you want to create. And behold, you are an artist. We are all artists. The inner canvas is the screen of your mind.

Unfortunately, the screen of our mind tends to be fully occupied by re-runs of the past or projections of possible futures. All the while your heart is patiently waiting to speak to you about wise and beautiful things but it cannot get through. The reason? Noise.

We spend most of our lives either creating or consuming a noise called thoughts. Sometimes we try to do both at the same time. The world out there has been getting noisier and noisier. We get busy converting that noise into thoughts. And those thoughts get mixed up with thoughts from memories and experiences. This makes it hard to even get started on our journey back to inner peace, calm, and contentment. Don't get the wrong idea, the aim is not to shut out the world, to try to avoid the sounds of our modern age, or even to stop thinking (at least at this stage). The aim is simply to increase the volume of your own inner quietness to give yourself the chance to connect to your well-spring of inner

power and hear what your heart has to say (sometimes called intuition). This is not an instant process. It takes a little practice. Here's how.

Begin by speaking less throughout your average day. Do you have to say everything you say? No! So cut out what you don't need to say. Then, after a few days, focus on saying what you do say more softly, and more slowly. When you do this you will begin to rediscover an inner rhythm, which is more like your natural rhythm. You will know it. You will begin to feel more comfortable and at ease with yourself, and with others. When you do these three things – speak less, speak softly, and speak slowly – your mind will do the same in your conversation with yourself. You will notice how much calmer you are, and how much more energy you have at your disposal. You will also begin to see both the quantity and the quality of your ideas increasing, and your capacity to discern and decide becoming sharper and easier. And you will have made an excellent start towards enlightenment in action.

If you explore the experiences of the mystics down through the ages, almost each and every one of them pointed towards silence as both the journey and the inner destination of an enlightened soul. An unchanging, still, silent being awaits each one of us at the heart of our own consciousness. It is where we find our true self, free of all mental pollution. It is where we find real peace and power. And when we have found our inner peace and our inner power we cannot help but transmit it into our relationships and into the world. This is why silence is the language of the soul. This is why true love, which is also silent, is the language of the heart.

BALM OF CALM

Watch what happens when you walk into a library or a meditation room. Notice how you are touched by the atmosphere, how you are influenced by the all-pervasive peacefulness. And in a few moments see how you are also beginning to be more mentally and intellectually peaceful. Then reflect on how the creation of such an atmosphere can create the balm of calm for others. Now think about your office, your lounge, and your community. Experiment. Be peaceful in your office or at home and watch how it influences others to join you. This is what makes creating peace within ourselves one of the greatest things we can do for others. Just as all objects are surrounded by space, so we are surrounded by silence. Between the notes of the symphony is silence, behind the painting is the empty silent canvas, and between our thoughts, and behind our thoughts, is silence. Be silent and calm and your vibration will create an atmosphere of calm silence. Others will feel it and it will help them to be it.

The 2nd AHA!

Let Go

All suffering and sorrow have the same cause – attachment. Don't become attached to anything.

Just as the bird has to find the courage to let go of the branch in order to fly, so we also need to let go of our branches if we are to know the exhilaration of soaring to our highest potential. The branches we hold on to are our attachments on the inside – our beliefs, ideas, and memories. And then there are the outer attachments – people, possessions, positions and privileges are a few. But as long as we hold on to any of them in our minds we will live in fear (of letting go and therefore loss or damage) and we will never be free. And just watch those birds; by letting go of one branch they are able to spend the rest of their lives alighting on a million other branches to enjoy the view from each. Are you flying and soaring in your life, or are you stuck on one branch, cursing others as they fly past? Go on, try it. Let go!

"But how?" you say. "I have been taught to hold on to stuff all my life, and now you say let go!" I don't mean physically, I mean mentally. Notice how everything comes to pass. Everything comes and eventually goes. I'm not saying you should start giving everything away. All that you have now, all that is in your life today, has come to you for you to 'use', for purposeful use, but not for holding on to. If you do try to hold on, to possess, even with your mind, you will generate fear: and remember, fear is stress, fear is pain. However, we have been wrongly taught that fear is a good, healthy, and necessary emotion for survival, so we do little to understand it, and even less to free ourselves from it. Fear eventually kills the creator of the fear – that's you! That's why almost all disease has a psychosomatic factor...and fear is it! All fear has its roots in attachment, in mentally holding on to something or somebody.

All you have to do is remember two things. One: It is not possible for the soul, that's you again, to possess anything, and two: If you don't let go, nothing new can show up. If the water does not leave the glass there is no room for fresh water. So how do you get started? Write down all your attachments – internal (beliefs, ideas, and memories) and the external (objects, people, places). Take one at a time and ask yourself what would life be like without them, rehearse your life without them, become accustomed to life without them. They will still be there but you will no longer hold on so tightly and fear will be no more. Now you are learning the most valuable art of all enlightenment schools – detachment.

Three things to remember:

1 Don't expect instant success. Don't beat yourself up when you notice how attached you are to something. Stay chilled. It takes time to heal the habits of a lifetime. The most common habit formed in everyone's lifetime is to become attached and therefore dependent on something or someone for our happiness, peace, and contentment. This is what makes us all suffer dozens of times a day. And then we mistakenly say, "Ah well, that's life, it's natural to be unhappy sometimes". No it's not! Wrong beliefs! The truth is, you neither own or possess anything. You need nothing to be truly happy. That is exactly why you often notice that those with less have a deeper and more consistent contentment than those with more!

2 Never lose sight of the result of learning detachment – freedom from fear in all its forms.

3 Watch out for one of those paradoxes – the more you let go/release the more people, opportunities, and ideas come to you!

Please don't go and give everything away to test this particular AHA! (well, a few bits and pieces perhaps!). The moment you become aware of the dead end and the suffering which comes with attachment, dependency, ownership, and possession you will begin to see many opportunities in your life to make detachment a reality. Letting go does not change your position, alter your pay or diminish the objects in your life. They are all there and still important, but your new relationship with them is what sets you free.

IN TRUST I DO HOLD!

So how do you overcome the illusion of ownership, which lies behind the impulse to possess and the habit of becoming attached to people and things? It's simple really. All you have to do is change your relationship with what you are attached to from owner/possessor to trustee. And that happens first in your head, and only then in your hands. And then, when whatever you are a trustee of (which is everything in your life right now) is relieved of your company, there will be no pain, no sorrow, only an easy release, accompanied by a natural acceptance and a quiet serenity. Possess nothing, hold everything in trust, and let go when the moment calls, and true freedom will be your companion.

The 3RD AHA!

Let Be

Interference is futile, it only results in absence!

Most of us are so busy interfering in the lives of others, either in our minds or in our conversations, that we forget to interfere in our own life and consciously create it here and now. This is why many of us spend most of our lives trying to live someone else's life. We are great fixers, and as we watch others we can hear ourselves attempting to sort them out in our own heads: "They shouldn't...weren't they awful...did you hear about so and so...in my opinion they should....I just can't understand how they could..." In these moments we waste time trying to write the script of others, and we forget to write our own. We have no right to write another's script, and any attempt to do so is futile, frustrating, and doomed to failure. So let be, learn to value the freedom from the tensions and anxieties about other people. Let them write their own script. Don't miss your life by trying to live someone else's, even for a few minutes.

Why do we all fall into this trap? Most of us are taught two fatal beliefs when we are young. One is that we can control others. And the second belief is that others are responsible for how we feel. But now you are enlightened. You know it is futile to try to control others and that you are the creator of your own feelings no matter what is happening around you. (At least in theory, it may take a little practice to make it a reality). So don't interfere with others' journeys, unless you are invited. Don't get involved in others' dramas unless you are invited. And if you are invited, be careful not to identify with their lives and the challenges that they face. Stand back a little, stay a little detached, and your contribution, when you are invited, will have much greater value.

Even if you are a parent you have no right to control the life of your children. That's not the purpose of parenthood. You offer an opportunity to the soul that is your child to learn and grow under your caring wings. You have a responsibility for their physical needs, to help them make sense of the world and then find their own way in the world, and to be themselves. Not to be what you want them to be. This is your opportunity to play mentor, coach, friend, companion, parent, and teacher. And in so doing the child becomes the teacher, the parent becomes the student, life becomes the school, the home is a classroom and the exams come thick and fast!

So next time you find yourself in a conversation that begins to generate judgments of others, be aware and be quiet. Quietly retire from the topic and learn the art of shifting focus. At first you will find this art quite challenging, especially in the company of people you know well. Shift focus to what? Try taking it inside instead of outside. Not with the aim of dumping your feelings or imposing your thoughts, but by sharing what you are learning from life, how you are enjoying the challenge of growing. You are learning, changing, and growing, aren't you? As you do this you will begin to recognize the moments when it is more appropriate to ask instead of tell, to inquire instead of impose, to listen instead of talk, to reflect instead of reinforce and in so doing lead your conversational companion into the territory of themselves, so that they may also learn, change, and grow. See how subtle leadership can be!

COMPASSION AND REVENGE

As you learn to let be you quickly realize the power in the art of acceptance. Everyone and everything is just as it is meant to be right now, and at every moment. However, when you see someone doing something morally wrong, like killing another person, do you just sit there and accept it and let it flow by? Is that a good moment to let be? If the event is in your lounge, obviously not. But be careful, the two main response options are the path of revenge or the path of compassion. When you want revenge you are saying you identified with another person's pain, and you are now in pain yourself, whereas when you choose compassion you are saying you understand the perpetrator is in pain and needs help. The path of compassion is always the most enlightened, but only when it results in the appropriate action. The path of revenge only sustains the pain for all, and two pains can never make a pleasure! The pain is also greatest for the one who chose revenge. When you walk the path of compassion you are demonstrating love in action and there is a greater chance of healing.

The 4th AHA!

Listen In

Your inner tutor is always available to you.

As human beings we have one thing in common – we are all unique! Each one of us is simply a being of consciousness within a human form – everything else, including race, nationality, profession, belief system, or religion is created, learned, and misused to generate our sense of identity. At the core of your consciousness, at the heart of your being, is your conscience. Consciousness, self and heart are synonymous. Your conscience is your receptacle of truth and wisdom, which lies at the core of your heart, not your physical heart, but the heart of your consciousness. We innately know who we really are and what is truly right. However, over time, all our externally focused learning, experiencing, and creating, sometimes called our conditioning, leaves us disconnected from the voice of truth within. Sometimes this voice speaks to you and you might even say, "Oh dear, my conscience is bothering me" or "I don't know why, but something tells me this is the wrong thing to do."

Like most people you may have a tendency to ignore this voice, sometimes deliberately drowning it out, especially if you know it will lead you away from what you think will give you pleasure, feed a dependency, or sustain an attachment. Every time you ignore it, suppress it, or drown it, you only hurt yourself, and eventually that pain will emerge as explosive emotion, negative feelings, or dysfunctional behavior. Much misery can be laid at the door of ignorance...in other words, the ignoring of the voice of your own innate truth, which is the core of your conscience.

And so it's time to heal and hear your still, small voice within. It's time to learn how to love and respect what is sometimes referred to as your 'inner child' – the pure, innocent, and unconditionally loving aspect within your being that has been neglected and ignored for too long. However, you will need to create a certain deep, inner quietness for the process of listening and healing to begin.

Only when you create this quietness in your own mind can you begin to hear your inner teacher, so that you may receive some in-tuition. Only when you are ready to recognize and value the wisdom you carry at the core of your being, will you 'be quiet' turn your attention inwards and 'listen in'. But it's been a long time since you truly listened and deeply trusted yourself, so a little practice and patience will be needed. Sit down, be quiet, and listen in at some point today, and you might be surprised at what you hear. Then do it again tomorrow. All you need to do is remember you are the listener and not the noise. You are the thinker, not the thoughts. You are the creator, the life-giver to your thoughts; you are not your thoughts. You are silent, your thoughts and feelings are the noise. The moment you separate yourself from your thoughts or feelings you instantly reconnect with your peace and you will begin to hear the voice of your innate wisdom.

Now consult your voice of wisdom. Place before it an important question or a difficult decision. Don't demand an answer, never struggle or wrestle to get some kind of reply. Pose the question, live in the question for a few moments, then go on your way, carry on with another task. At the right moment the answer will occur, the insight will appear in your mind. And you will think or even say, "AHA!" But still the job is not complete – now extend that moment into an inward gesture of appreciation and gratitude for this clarity. In this way you melt the barriers between you and truth, you and wisdom, you and your self! Then enlightenment will always only be one second away.

And if, when you get an answer, there is still some doubt, then consult a source you recognize as experienced and wise. Check to see if your voice has been distorted by fear or hatred. If it has, then further patient listening is required alongside the recognition and the healing of your fears and hatreds.

OASIS MOMENTS

As most of us live each day in perpetual motion we seldom allow time for ourselves. Time for our self does not mean reading the paper or hanging out in the bar. It means sitting quietly, being quiet and being with one's self. Be ruthless with your diary, put yourself down for three or four oasis moments every day. Then give yourself the gifts of meditation and reflection, which are the proven way to restore inner peace and inner power. Don't think about it. Just do it!

The 5th AHA!

Accept Everything

Resist nothing because it only strengthens what you resist and prolongs the struggle.

Have you ever noticed how resistance leads to persistence? Whatever you resist or push against simply persists and pushes back in equal measure. It seems to be one of those iron-clad laws within our energetic universe. Whether it's one on one, community against community, nation against nation – when one pushes against the other, or resists the position of the other, there is something called continuous conflict. We all find occasion to reject and resist another person. We all like to put up a fight from our armchair against anything we dislike on the evening news as we watch the world. But we forget that when we decide to resist something or somebody, either mentally or physically, we only empower the object of our resistance, either in reality, or in our own minds. Mental, and therefore emotional, resistance then becomes a habit.

It's all because we have a subconscious belief that the world should sing our song and when it doesn't our anger turns into more resistance. And when we create resistance towards anything or anyone, we automatically create our own fear. Actually, it's only and always fear which lies behind all our resistant behaviors. It's all coming from that belief that we can and should control what we cannot control, that the world should dance to our tune.

If, on the other hand, you want to enjoy the ability to influence people and situations, always start with acceptance. If you want to disarm another, begin with acceptance. If you want to encourage and empower another to change, start with acceptance. If you want to resolve conflict in any relationship, begin with acceptance. If you are going to be a leader, always begin with acceptance. Don't make it conditional. Otherwise it's just resistance disguised as acceptance, you are still trying to control others, and you are still scared. Acceptance connects you with the energy of the person or the flow of the situation, and when you connect and flow you will have maximum influence. But as soon as you resist you disconnect, you find yourself trying to control, and barriers go up immediately.

And so it is within. You already are peaceful, patient, and wise at heart. Struggling to defeat the habits of fear and anger only sustains and strengthens these habits, and thereby strengthens the barrier between you and your peace, between you and your wisdom, between you and your power to be patient. If there is any struggle in your effort to change yourself, then it's as if you are resisting what you want to change within yourself. These will also be habits you have created in the past. Remember, you are not your habits, but you tend to identify with your habits, sometimes saying to yourself that they are 'my nature', so that the moment you struggle and therefore resist a habit it's if you are resisting yourself. You are in effect battling with yourself. This then makes the habit you are trying to change even stronger, drains the power, and weakens your ability to establish new patterns of positive thought and behavior.

This resistance of yourself, within the struggle to change yourself, only leads to suppression and the build up of buried emotional energy in your subconscious. It's only a matter of time before it explodes. The deepest secret of all inner change and healing is self-acceptance, not self-resistance, and certainly not self-rejection. We are all taught to reject ourselves in some way or other, usually in our childhood, but we are not aware of it at the time. As soon

as one of those big important people in our young life rejects us, or rejects themselves and thereby teaches us how to do it to ourselves, the voice of self-rejection occupies our inner ear for the rest of our lives. It also teaches us to reject others, which can become fatal in our relationships. So whatever feelings come, whatever emotions emerge, learn to accept them. That begins with becoming aware of them, simply observing them, acknowledging them, and then accepting them. The result is integration. In reality, when you do this, you are really accepting yourself, and that is the beginning of loving yourself. And that is the beginning of healing.

Remember that acceptance is only the first step to transforming our unwanted habits of thought and/or emotion. The second step is detachment from the inner voice of self criticism and self rejection which is generating your resistance and therefore your fear. The third step is the focessed application of knowledge and wisdom to create a new pattern of thought, feeling and behaviour.

When you do recognise an unwanted or negative emotional state, be careful not to lose yourself in the emotion. That's not acceptance, that's indulgence, and once again only reinforcing the habit of creating the emotion. Accept the emotions that you feel, detach yourself from them, then simply observe the emotion and you will find the emotion will begin to dissolve. Emotion dies in the light of detached observation. Don't forget that true love is not an emotion! Love never dies, which is why there is no need to 'make love'! Love is already made, it only awaits expression.

MEDICATION AND MEDITATION

Just as we have the capacity to know and express love at three levels – physical, mental and spiritual – so we have the capacity to feel pain at these levels. Mental and emotional pain needs your attention because only you know what you are feeling, exactly why you are feeling it, and what needs to change. Spiritual pain needs to be understood and healed through the study of wisdom and the practice of meditation. Medication for the body, that's your vehicle, and meditation for the soul – that's you! Don't forget that the health of your body begins with and is sustained by the health of the soul/self. This is why you cannot afford the luxury of a negative thought!

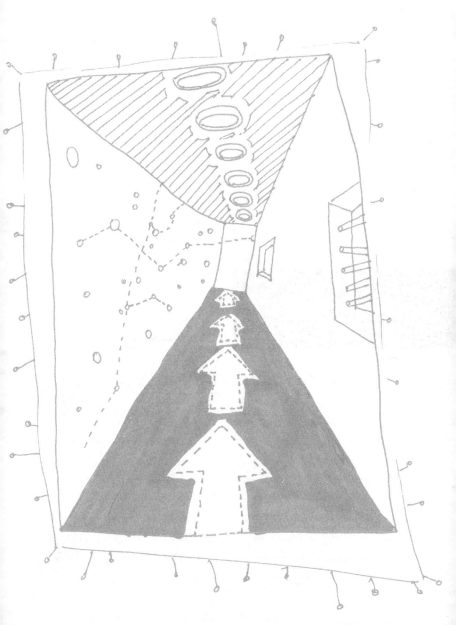

The 5th AHA! | 95

The 6th AHA!

Know Self

You cannot start living
'for real' until you know who
and what you are.

So who are you? Or what are you? Are you
what you do – as defined by your job title?
Are you where you come from, as defined by
your nationality? If you were born in a stable
does that make you a horse? Are you what
people call you – as defined by your name?
Are you what you believe – as defined by what
you may call your faith?   If none of these
things are what you are, which they aren't,
what are you? Who are you? There's nothing
left. So what shall we call you? Nothing? No
thing is better. But then what? Awareness?
Consciousness? Soul? Spirit? Or are these
just more labels? Can you go beyond all the
labels and just be your self? Self.   Individual.
Aware. Conscious. Free. Self-aware self.
That's what you are.   Try telling that to
passport control!

The common language of the world is the language of labels. And just as the labels on the box, or those hanging from the dress, are not the item that they describe, we have learned to mistake the two. We think we are what the label says. And then, when the label is threatened or moved we get very upset. We find it hard to see the illusion and realize that the truth is we are not what the label says. Some of us will die for their label, and some will even kill for their label. We are not our nationality, our gender, our race, or our religion. But we are taught to think we are, and that's extremely unen-lightened. It also makes life an extremely painful journey.

It's not surprising that those around us often know us better than we know ourselves. No one teaches us the value of getting to know the self. As a famous Greek philosopher once said, "the unexamined life is not worth living" – which really means that self is seldom fully known. To know oneself is to be aware of one's true identity (spirit) true nature (peace), and true purpose (creating, giving, and receiving). When this is experienced and known, you will then begin to understand where emotions like anger and depression, pain and discomfort, emptiness and greed come from. You need to know how and why these feelings surface in your personality, otherwise misery will visit you frequently, there will be an absence of meaning and you will feel that your life has no value.

Ask the question who and what am I, and why am I here? Then give yourself the gift of patience, listen to your intuition again, and all will become clear. If necessary, eliminate all the things you are not, which are all those labels mentioned earlier, and see what is left. Some people think that when you do this you lose your identity. You don't. You have already lost your identity in the numerous labels and compartments that you learn to mistakenly use to describe your self. When you drop all these false identities you will begin to regain an awareness of your true self. This awareness is much more of an experience than it is an idea, which is why meditation is the best way to reach it.

Unless you do this, unless you consciously set out to experience what you truly are, behind all the labels and false, transient identities, (position, nationality, belief systems, etc.) you may simply repeat the most frequent living pattern in human life today, where almost every human being is born, lives, and dies without ever knowing themselves.

Remember, how you see yourself completely influences how you see the world, what you think about the world and therefore what you give to the world. And what you give to the world is what you get back from the world. But you already know all that, don't you?

This is why identity is destiny.

TREASURE HUNT!

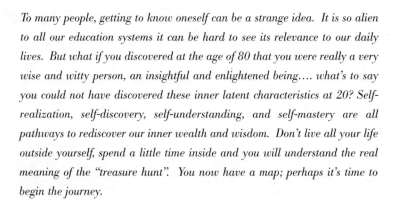

To many people, getting to know oneself can be a strange idea. It is so alien to all our education systems it can be hard to see its relevance to our daily lives. But what if you discovered at the age of 80 that you were really a very wise and witty person, an insightful and enlightened being…. what's to say you could not have discovered these inner latent characteristics at 20? Self-realization, self-discovery, self-understanding, and self-mastery are all pathways to rediscover our inner wealth and wisdom. Don't live all your life outside yourself, spend a little time inside and you will understand the real meaning of the "treasure hunt". You now have a map; perhaps it's time to begin the journey.

The 7th AHA!

7 Pass On

Everything comes to pass, it is for use, not possession, and passing everything on enhances the value of the passed and the passer.

Everything means every thing and everything that is not a thing! Not just the money in our pocket but wisdom, objects, ideas, even opportunities, all come to us so that, at the right moment, we can pass them on. This is called flow.

Awareness of flow means being aware that the river of life is flowing to us at every moment.

Going with the flow means accepting whatever comes, and putting it to good use… before passing it on.

Being in the flow means allowing whatever comes to move on freely, without being influenced or holding on in any way.

If you do not pass on whatever comes to you, then you are trying to block the flow of life and that's when you feel pressure. Pressure is always self-inflicted. Every time you feel yourself to be under pressure, look at what you need to pass on to someone else. What do you need to release, to let go, allow to move on? It could simply be the way you are thinking. Are you thinking negatively? If so, don't pass it on to someone else but instead to your inner rubbish bin. Then incinerate the rubbish. When you do, you will discover a quality of contentment and a kind of surrender that is one of the deepest and most profound forms of relaxation.

The river is the perfect metaphor for life. We are all in the "river of life", while each one of us is a river in our own right. What does the river do on its journey from mountain to ocean? What is its highest purpose? Yes, it does carve out its own path, it does carry things downstream; yes, it does provide a home for certain creatures; but its highest purpose is to nourish and sustain every living creature that it touches on its way to the ocean. The field, the flowers, the trees, the animals, and of course, you and I – we are each nourished by the river. It is the same with our own purpose in life. Why are you here? What are you here to do? To nourish and be nourished on your journey through life. The highest nourishment is wisdom and the highest wisdom in action is to give, without wanting anything in return. To pass on whatever has come to us, to others, and to the world.

This is why work is not work. When you enter your

place of work you are not there to do a job, get the money and run! You are there within a community of relationships to nourish and be nourished. To flow into and through the lives of others, to fulfil your highest purpose, if you so choose. All our relationships are such opportunities. They are opportunities to serve, to give, and to pass on what we hold in the hands of our mind and heart. You don't have to be a member of some religion or spiritual order to fulfil such an auspicious purpose. Simply be available for others, simply give more where you used to take, simply see everything and everyone in the river of life as your opportunity to nurture and nourish. Only then will you discover your life purpose, only then will you free yourself from the monkey on your shoulder, which has been asking almost every day, "What's the meaning of it all?" Only then will enthusiasm and energy begin to invade your heart. And only then will you find the greatest happiness, the truest love, and the deepest peace. Be a scientist tomorrow, try this 'passing on' experiment in the test tube of your day, and see the difference it makes.

OFFERINGS NOT IMPOSINGS!

Remember not to force or impose yourself or your gifts on others. Often they are not ready, or don't want to accept, so make your gifts invisible and intangible. Take one idea from this little book and give it to someone tomorrow – don't impose it on someone. Offer it, and give it only if the offer to share is accepted. In this way you give value to the time you spent reading, and you will never forget the idea that you shared, and you will have served another, touched and nourished another's heart with your own. In such meetings of hearts is the reason why we are here.

Why Enlightenment and Transformation does not happen... very quickly!

The drains are still open!

Ever wondered why the process of inner change is so slow? Ever wondered why, despite the wonderful books, seminars, and modern-day enlightenment gurus, all dispensing the deepest wisdom and universal truths in the most palatable ways, very few people are actually experiencing deep inner change? Here is why. It doesn't matter how much wisdom and insight that you consume, or how many tools or techniques that you master. It doesn't matter how many books you read, seminars that you attend, and treatments that you pay for. It won't make any difference unless you do what almost everyone does not want to do. And that is 'close the drains'.

So what are the drains? At the level of emotion, which is where we most frequently lose control of the energy of our consciousness, the drains are fear, anger, and depression. Unless we understand and free ourselves from fear, anger and depression then any serious inner personal transformation will not happen.

Wisdom, truth, and insight are all forms of power. As you read, hear, see, think about, and remember what is right and true, as you learn new inner skills to manage your life more effectively, you are empowering yourself. When the AHA! moment occurs you feel a surge of inner power. Hence, the most common feeling at the end of the book/seminar/consultation is the feeling of being uplifted. But unless you close the drains, that power will simply drain away in a matter of days, maybe hours.

Few of us want to work on the drains, few of us want to explore and understand their presence, simply because we have come to believe that their disturbances are OK, even good, useful, and of some value. But they are not. It is an illusion to think they have a place in our inner world. Fear, anger, and depression are the parent emotions to a hundred others including irritation, tension, excitement, hate, anxiety, insecurity, frustration, melancholy, etc. They have nothing to contribute to love, contentment, compassion, peace, or human happiness.

Our learned beliefs just don't like it when we come to realize that anger, fear, and sadness are disabling and disempowering us while they drain our spiritual and mental energy. We have been taught to believe anger is strength, when it is a weakness. Be aware of yourself immediately following an angry outburst, are you filled with power or are you drained? We have been taught to believe that fear is necessary to beat the deadline, to get things done, when in fact, it paralyses us. Be aware of yourself just after the deadline has passed, are you feeling powerful or drained? We have also learned to believe that sadness is an essential ingredient in a good story, so we expect and wallow in it as we watch a movie or listen to music. And how do you feel afterwards, empowered or drained? How can sadness uplift when it is the ultimate downer? In the world of human relationships, how can anger change anything for the better when its projection on to others invites the building of barriers and the creation of hate? How can fear be healthy when it makes our heart break its own speed limit, produce far too much adrenaline, and seriously damage our health?

But so attached are we to these beliefs, so attached are we to the emotional experiences which they sustain within us, we will fight to hold on to them. We will challenge anyone who dares to say these emotions not only drain our power, but also will eventually kill us if we continue to give them life inside our consciousness.

So it's simple really. If you consume a little wisdom and feel uplifted, that's good. If you "do" the empowerment seminar and feel empowered, that's great. If you experienced one or two AHA!s, that's wonderful, your time has been well spent. But don't forget to close the drains, (anger, fear, and sadness) or the power you have just replenished will simply drain away - again! Eliminate fear, banish anger, and let go of all your sadness! Then you will be moving on the road to enlightenment, ready to be reunited with your innate wisdom and your personal power.

How do you close the drains? If you really are serious about your own transformation, if you are genuinely interested in 'waking up', if you can decide now that you will have a love affair with truth, you will find out.

Start by reading this little book again. All the clues are there. Anything that is not clear, simply ask!

Starting Points

If there are two things I would love you to learn, only because I learned them many years ago and they changed my life, they are detachment and meditation. It is no accident that for 2,000 years these have been at the heart of personal enlightenment and self-empowerment. There is a simple way to begin each. Try them. Experience the peace and the power that they restore and then hunt down a meditation course and allow someone experienced to teach you.

You will never regret it.

Detachment – Stay in Your Chair

Next time you watch a movie don't 'go into' the movie, don't lose your self in the plot, don't identify with the characters, and don't allow your emotions to be manipulated. It's just a movie. Stay in your chair. Practice being a detached observer. Simply watch the drama unfold from a distance. This will help you to maintain your cool and calm in real-life situations when others lose theirs and want you to join them. Don't allow your rational mind to tell you that it is cold and unfeeling to be detached. It is not. In fact, it gives you the ability to see, understand, and respond with greater sensitivity when you don't identify with other's emotions and become embroiled in their side of their story. It allows you to remain clear-headed and focused. It also helps you to help others when they are being ruled by their emotions. This is the art of detached observation and detached involvement. You will find this a priceless ability.

Meditation – Try This

Stop what you are doing. Find a quiet corner. Sit comfortably. Acknowledge and relax your body. Become aware of your mental activity. Observe your thoughts and feelings – become a witness to them. As you observe and witness your thoughts and feelings you may sometimes feel the temptation to be drawn into them. If you do, then gently release them and return to the observer position. Now carefully move your observer awareness until you can see the space between your thoughts. As you do this you will begin to experience an inner peace gradually building within your consciousness. The more you try this, the more powerful and concentrated that peacefulness will become. With regular practice you will be able to do it anywhere, anytime. You will begin to see the events around you with greater clarity and you will start to hear your own wisdom speak from the heart of your consciousness. Both that clarity and wisdom will help you to build your capacity to make your life meaningful and purposeful. This is the beginning of meditation. Patience is the key. The power of concentration and creativity are the eventual rewards.

One Final Thought

The announcement came as an item in the news only recently. Scientists had just discovered what might be the ultimate self-help cure for cancer. At a research laboratory they had taken seratonin, which is the hormone produced by the brain when we are happy, placed it in a test tube of cancer cells, and it had instantly killed every cell. Asked why it had taken so long to make this discovery, their reply was simple, "There are a million chemicals which could be tested on cancer and we have only just got round to trying seratonin".

So there you are, scientific proof that happiness heals. It may be a new truth to the world of science, but it is not new to many who have intuitively known for a very long time.

Remember, happiness is not a dependency, it is a decision. Happiness is not a destination, it is the journey. Happiness is not an achievement, it is the way to achieve. Happiness never waits, it is now or it is never. Delay no longer. Be happy now. The world is waiting for the serenity of your smile, the contentment of your heart, and the echoes of your laughter.

About the Author

Based in London and the Cotswolds, Mike George plays a variety of roles including spiritual teacher, motivational speaker, retreat leader and management development tutor/facilitator. In a unique blend of insight, wisdom and humour, Mike brings together the three key strands of the new millennium –

emotional/spiritual intelligence
management/leadership development
and continuous learning.

Working with people within companies and communities in over thirty countries his workshops, seminars and retreats are primarily designed to help people:

- Raise awareness of their own inner resources so they may be more content within themselves and more effective in all that they do.
- Develop the practical emotional and spiritual skills to build and sustain stable and loving relationships.
- Discover and explore the essential wisdom which they need to create a more balanced and contented life.

Retreats and workshops include Self Awareness and Personal Enlightenment; Liberating Leadership; Mastering Deep Change; Working with Emotional Intelligence; Conflict Resolution; Meditation and the Art of Heart Maintenance. His clients range across private and public sectors and include Mitsubishi, American Express, Siemens, Allianz, Barclays Bank, Johnson and Johnson, KLM Royal Dutch Airlines, the NHS, Help the Aged and the BBC.

For the last twenty years he has also traveled extensively teaching the art of meditation and assisting others in their spiritual development. His other publications include:

Learn to Relax
(Duncan Baird/UK & Chronicle/USA)

Learn to Find Inner Peace
(Duncan Baird/UK & Chronicle/USA)

The Secrets of Self Management
(BK Publications)

Meditation for Extremely Busy People
(BK Publications)

Stress Free Living
(BK Publications)

In the Light of Meditation
(O-Books)

He is the managing editor of Heart & Soul Magazine and the founder of The Relaxation Centre. (relax7.com)

Mike can be contacted at
mike@relax7.com

For a diary of lectures, talks, workshops, seminars and retreats see www.relax7.com/diary

Thanks and Links

Thanks to the Global Retreat Centre and
the Brahma Kumaris World Spiritual University for the
context and the wisdom.

www.globalretreatcentre.com
www.bkwsu.org.uk

Thanks to Reed Learning for the opportunity to 'pass
on' to others

www.reed.co.uk/learning

Thanks to Bliss for the kind of music that relaxes and
induces quiet moments for inspiration and the
occasional AHA!

www.blissfulmusic.com

Thanks to Kenwood House at Hampstead Heath for the
desk in the sun and the best cappuccino in town.

Thanks and buckets of love to all my sisters and
brothers for your ever-present subtle support.